WINNING SPIRIT BASKETBALL

FIND YOUR GREATNESS WITHIN

WINNING SPIRIT BASKETBALL

FIND YOUR GREATNESS WITHIN

CHRIS MULLIN
TOM MITCHELL

SPORTS
PUBLISHING

Sports Publishing books may be purchased in bulk at special discounts for
sales promotion, corporate gifts, fund-raising, or educational purposes. Special
editions can also be created to specifications. For details, contact the Special Sales
Department, Sports Publishing, 307 West 36th Street, 11th Floor, New York, NY
10018 or sportspubbooks@skyhorsepublishing.com.

Sports Publishing® is a registered trademark of Skyhorse Publishing, Inc.®, a
Delaware corporation.

Visit our website at www.sportspubbooks.com.

10 9 8 7 6 5 4 3 2 1

Library of Congress Cataloging-in-Publication Data is available on file.

ISBN: 978-1-61321-313-1

Printed in China

DEDICATED TO THE
YOUNG AT HEART WHO LOVE
THE GAME OF BASKETBALL.

CONTENTS

Introduction by Chris Mullin. 1

Introduction by Tom Mitchell 3

CHAPTER 1   A Burning Desire. 7

CHAPTER 2   Love the Game. 11

CHAPTER 3   Your Home Team. 15

CHAPTER 4   Compete with the Best 19

CHAPTER 5   The Power of the Pen. 23

CHAPTER 6   It's Your Life. 27

CHAPTER 7   The Inner Game 31

CHAPTER 8   Practice Time. 35

CHAPTER 9   Feel the Flow 39

CHAPTER 10   A Coach's Dream 43

CHAPTER 11   Breaking a Sweat 47

CHAPTER 12   Free Your Mind 51

CHAPTER 13   Confidence Comes from Within 55

CHAPTER 14   Welcome Pressure 59

CHAPTER 15   Beginner's Mind. 63

CHAPTER 16   Positive Words 67

CHAPTER 17   Talk with Your Coach 71

CHAPTER 18   Your Inner Circle 75

CHAPTER 19   Emotions Are Real 79

CHAPTER 20   Right Here, Right Now 83

CHAPTER 21   Have Courage 93

CHAPTER 22   Express Yourself. 97

CHAPTER 23   Have Fun. 101

CHAPTER 24   The Inner Coach 105

CHAPTER 25   Beyond the Score. 109

CHAPTER 26   Fear as an Advantage 113

CHAPTER 27   Learn from Loss. 117

CHAPTER 28   Protect Yourself 121

CHAPTER 29   Walk in Their Shoes. 125

CHAPTER 30   Evaluate Yourself 129

CHAPTER 31   Playing in the Moment 133

CHAPTER 32   A Powerful Imagination. 137

CHAPTER 33   Relax 141

CHAPTER 34   Never Give Up. 145

CHAPTER 35   Appreciate It All. 149

CHAPTER 36   Ask for Help 153

CHAPTER 37   Go Beyond Your Comfort Zone . . 157

CHAPTER 38   Celebrate Success. 161

CHAPTER 39   Giving Back. 165

CHAPTER 40   Honor the Game 169

Acknowledgements. 173

INTRODUCTION

CHRIS MULLIN

Over the years, Tom and I have talked for hours about the subjects that we write about in our book, *Winning Spirit Basketball*. Not only as a former professional athlete, but also as a father of four, I have found that the topics presented here are essential for players, parents, and coaches.

This is not a book about the Xs and Os of basketball. You will not learn how to run a play, shoot a free throw, or break a full court press. Rather, you will learn about the values within the game of basketball that help you become a better player on the court and a better person in life. Through very basic and easy-to-understand messages and exercises, you will be able to put the things you learn from this book into practice immediately.

It has been my experience that basketball is a great way to build character, have fun, learn about other people, and develop confidence. These are the things I have tried to teach and instill into my own children every day. These are the most important, fundamental qualities that any athlete can possess.

INTRODUCTION

TOM MITCHELL

Winning Spirit Basketball grew out of conversations with Chris Mullin about players, coaches and the game of basketball. It is written specifically for basketball players who want to gain a competitive edge and a better understanding of the habits and behaviors that are at the heart of an athlete's success: confidence, communication, work ethic, teamwork, practice and concentration. We also feel it is vital to encourage players to strive for excellence in other areas of their lives as well.

Winning Spirit Basketball can also be useful for parents who want to support their children or coaches who want to help their players develop their mental game.

You can read this book straight through or randomly choose any chapter you'd like. Each chapter stands alone and contains a message and an activity to practice and think about. Several chapters have similar themes, but require you to look at them in different ways.

Have fun working with this book. Focus on each chapter and take the time to let the messages sink in. Strive for success both on and off the court!

WINNING SPIRIT
BASKETBALL

FIND YOUR
GREATNESS
WITHIN

1

A BURNING DESIRE

If you want to be a really good player, a burning desire is the most important quality you can have. Desire is an inner energy that gives you the drive and passion to improve. It's an intensity that burns inside. Some days, all you can think about is being out on the court; some nights, you lay awake, practicing moves over and over in your mind. You think about the next game with great anticipation.

Desire gives you the motivation to get in great shape. It drives you to keep developing your talent. It is the motivation to constantly practice your shooting, ball handling, and passing skills. Great players cannot have too much desire.

Pure desire comes from within, pushing you onward to discover how good you can be. Your path to greatness can be encouraged by others but cannot come from another person. It can only come from you.

Use this burning desire and turn it into concentration and dedication to see how good you can become.

I HAVE A BURNING DESIRE
TO IMPROVE EVERY DAY.

PRACTICE THIS

Get a half-dozen 3 by 5 cards. On each card, write down what you want to accomplish in basketball. It should be the one most important thing you desire to achieve this season. Keep it very simple, using only a few words to say what you really want.

Then, put one card in a place where you will see it every day. Continue placing the other 5 cards in private places where you will see them often. These cards will serve as daily reminders to focus on your goal.

2

LOVE THE GAME

The greatest thing about playing basketball is that you get to participate in a game that is unbelievably fun. Playing isn't an obligation; it is something you want to do! Playing basketball is one of your favorite things to do. Everyone who loves basketball knows that feeling when you just can't get enough. You can't wait to get on the court and when it's time to leave, you don't want to. Whether outside or in a gym, there is no place that you would rather be.

However, as time goes on, there may be days when the routine of practice gets tough. The pressure of and commitment to the season can set in and you feel burnt out. You could even lose some of your competitive drive.

This is natural and happens to everyone from time to time. If this happens to you, remember why you fell in love with the game in the first place and why you play. Think about all of the good things that basketball gives you and play it with all your heart.

I LOVE THIS GAME! I GIVE IT EVERYTHING I'VE GOT.

PRACTICE THIS

When it comes to basketball, eliminate saying "I have to" and replace it with saying "I want to." In your day-to-day life, there are probably enough "I have to" responsibilities and obligations. Remember basketball is a game, not a job!

When you go to practice, remind yourself it is something you want to do, not something you have to do. Think and say, "I want to practice really hard to improve. I want to put in extra time and effort. I want to be coached. I'm on the court because it's something I really love to do."

3

YOUR HOME TEAM

Who are people that you depend on to make your basketball experience possible? What roles do they play? They could be your parents, grandparents, brothers, sisters, friends, or anyone you rely on.

Some members of your home team cook for you, wash your clothes, and help take care of your everyday needs. Others may drive you to practice and games. These teammates devote many hours of their time to you. They sit in the stands to watch and cheer. Others teach skills that help you on the court. Some of these loyal teammates give comfort when you are down or hurt. They give advice when you need guidance and direction.

Take a moment to realize how fortunate you are to have even one person that helps you in this way. Isn't it awesome that these people care so much about you? Go out of your way to thank them for giving of their time and energy. Tell them how much you love them. Appreciate your home team; they are a huge part of your success.

MY HOME TEAM IS A HUGE
PART OF MY SUCCESS.

CHRIS MULLIN AND TOM MITCHELL

PRACTICE THIS

Make a list of every member of your home team. Then, write each one of them a thank-you card. In it, tell them how important playing basketball is to you.

In your own words, tell them how much you appreciate what they are doing for you. Your words and thoughtfulness will show them that all of their effort is worth it.

Don't hold back. Be sure they know how thankful you really are. Maybe you have already told them this before, but it is always good to get such a sincere and considerate message. They will treasure it for years to come.

4

COMPETE WITH THE BEST

It is a great feeling to compete against players who have skill and talent better than your own. This kind of competition shows you how good you really are. When you come face to face with teams and players who may be better, you learn a lot about yourself. These opponents can become some of your best teachers.

To really discover your greatness, you need to test yourself with the toughest competition you can find. In the off-season, whether in a league, with older kids at the park, or playing one-on-one in your driveway, play with the best. After all, it is easy to feel confident when you play against those teams and players who have less talent and ability. But when you play against the best teams and players, you will be challenged to dig deep inside and see what you are made of.

PLAYING AGAINST
THE BEST...
BRINGS OUT MY BEST.

PRACTICE THIS

Below, you will be asked to think about your toughest competitors and which players challenge you the most. As you think about your answers, develop a feeling of respect for your competition. Try not to be intimidated by them. Rather, appreciate that their toughness and desire to win actually helps you to become a tougher and more competitive player.

> » Who are the toughest competitors you play with or against?
> » Why do you like to compete?

5

THE POWER OF THE PEN

It is a good practice to keep a record of your basketball progress. It will help you become clearer about what you want to accomplish on and off the court. You may find that writing down your thoughts increases your motivation and confidence. Writing often makes things more "real." Your desire and emotion can come through and the power of your own words can inspire you.

Write down your goals, successes and achievements, fears and failures. Capture good times you have had with your coaches, teammates, and friends. Whenever a new idea pops into your head, write it down. Also, writing down your goals can remind you of and reinforce what you really want.

Every now and then, reread the things you have written. This practice can become a good aid to you in the days to come. Remember, you are worth writing about!

WRITING DOWN MY GOALS
HELPS ME TO KNOW WHAT I WANT.

PRACTICE THIS

The questions and activities in this book are designed to get you to think and feel more deeply about basketball. They will also help you to understand yourself better as an athlete and as a person. Have fun thinking about the questions and writing down your answers.

» What is the most important goal you have for this season?

6

IT'S YOUR LIFE

Although being an athlete and playing basketball may be where your head is now and what you are currently enjoying the most, you are much, much more than just a basketball player. Your life includes so many other potential areas of interest, such as developing solid relationships with friends and family, making a difference in the lives of others, and learning new things about the world. There are so many directions you can go. Basketball is only a part of a full, rich life.

Develop yourself as a person as well as a an athlete. Be curious and make a commitment to be good at many things.

Look for athletes who have the desire to excel in both their sport and studies. Hang out with friends that are loyal. Surround yourself with the best quality people you can find. Strive to become a well-rounded person. Believe in yourself and know you are capable of great things both on and off the court.

I STRIVE TO BE A
WELL-ROUNDED PERSON.

PRACTICE THIS

Ask your family members and good friends what they like and appreciate about you the most. Ask them what they think your best qualities are. Make sure that you write down their answers. Do not be surprised if they don't even talk about you as a basketball player.

» Did anyone say anything that surprised you? What was it? Why were you surprised?

7

THE INNER GAME

The final outcome of any game or any season is always uncertain, but feeling a sense of satisfaction is possible every game. The *inner game win* depends on you and not the final score. Sure, every basketball player wants to win every game, including the ultimate championship. But when it's said and done, all teams but one will have lost their final game of the season. Winning the championship or coming in first place does not guarantee that you have the ultimate feeling of success.

The *inner game win* will happen when you *know* that you have given your very best effort and made no excuses. When you play with heart and commitment, stay focused, know your role, make those around you better, and never give up, you will earn a real feeling of personal pride no matter what the final score is. Coaches, teammates, and even opponents will respect you because they recognize that you play with an intense competitive spirit and have an attitude of a winner.

THERE IS MORE TO BASKETBALL
THAN THE FINAL SCORE.

PRACTICE THIS

Think about a time when you played with so much intensity and focus, so much effort and energy that you did not even think about the score. Was there ever a time when you became so completely absorbed in the game that the score was not the only important thing?

> » What does winning mean to you?
> » It may be a good idea to write down your own, unique definition of winning.

PRACTICE TIME

For you to become a great basketball player, you must learn to practice with great concentration. You must bring your best energy and effort to the gym every day.

Practice is your time to work on many of your skills. The more you practice with dedication and focus, the more quickly you improve. If you want to develop a new skill, put in extra practice. Remember, repetition is king. Do more than is required and you'll feel good about yourself.

Practicing with your team is best because you get to play with friends that have the same goal as you. It is fun when you push your teammates and they push you to get better.

Always be open to the suggestions and critique of your coaches. It is their job to make sure that you are developing good habits. Listen carefully to what they say.

Also, spend as much time as you can practicing alone. Practicing alone shows that you are motivated to improve and that you love basketball.

I PRACTICE WITH CONCENTRATION
AND INTENSITY.

PRACTICE THIS

The next time you go to practice, go with the motivation to improve! Even if you pick just one drill, work on it with 100% concentration. Keep working on it, over and over, until you know you are getting better. Remember, repetition is king. You don't have to be perfect. It's all about improving. There is nothing like a good, intense practice.

» What do you think your coach would say your attitude is like in practice?
» What motivates you to practice really hard?

FEEL THE FLOW

When you're a creative player, you play with a sense of freedom. You have your own unique style. Although you need to be a team player, you are an individual. No one plays the game exactly like you.

Creativity is the blending of your skill, instincts, and intelligence. When you are creative, you still play with good fundamentals and allow the game to come to you without trying too hard. You play freely and fearlessly, but with discipline and control.

Playing creatively does not necessarily mean being fancy. It means that you create your own style to get the job done. That may mean giving a head fake, going behind your back, or being crafty with the ball.

Work on finding your feeling of flow and balance. Experience that place known as "the zone," where you find your rhythm and the game comes to you easily. Think of basketball as an art as well as a sport. Let the court become your canvas and the game, your masterpiece.

I FEEL THE FLOW AND
RHYTHM OF THE GAME.

PRACTICE THIS

Go to a gym or an outside court where you like to play. Bring some music that really makes you feel like moving. Pick a move that you want to work on and then, almost in slow motion, with the music playing, begin working on it.

Be aware of every aspect of your move. Pay attention to how your body feels. Concentrate on fine-tuning it. Begin picking up pace and speed as you go. After a while, switch to another move and do the same thing. Feel the flow and release the creative part of yourself.

10

A Coach's Dream

If you work hard, listen well, and have a burning desire to improve, you are a coach's dream. Every coach loves a player with this kind of attitude.

When you are a coach's dream, you make no excuses about the past, but give your full attention to today. You give everything you have during practice and in games, which not only impresses your coach, but also inspires your team.

When you are a coach's dream, you understand the word commitment. You dedicate a lot of your time to basketball and give up other activities. Your actions on and off the court show how much you care.

When you are a coach's dream, you focus on making your teammates better. You put the team first. You are looked at as a leader because you have the courage to deal with tough situations. You know there is no challenge too big to handle because you have the mental toughness necessary to get the job done.

I WORK HARD TO
EARN THE CONFIDENCE
OF MY COACH.

PRACTICE THIS

Ask a coach about a player in the past with an outstanding attitude, a player who would be considered a coach's dream. Ask them to tell you a story or share an example about this player. What made them stand out in comparison to other players? What special qualities did they possess? This exercise will help you better understand what it takes to be thought of as a coach's dream.

» If you were a coach, what kind of player would you want on your team?
» Are you a coach's dream?

11

BREAKING A SWEAT

If you really want to become a great player, you need to understand that "there is no substitute for hard work." If being a great player came easily, without tremendous dedication and work, it wouldn't mean much. Basketball would not be as challenging nor success as sweet.

When you want to be an outstanding player, hard work is not only necessary; it is something you do with pride. As you put in hour after hour of practice and push yourself to the limit, you will gain a feeling of deep satisfaction.

When you feel this, you will understand why there is no substitute for hard work. You may be working on shooting, ball handling, passing, defense, or any other part of your game. Whatever it is, working hard on the court is one of the best feelings in the world!

Your desire to excel makes you stand out. When you work hard, you gain immediate respect from teammates, other players, coaches, and everyone who watches you. Most important, you feel good about yourself.

I STRIVE TO BE THE HARDEST
WORKER ON MY TEAM.

PRACTICE THIS

Go to a gym or a park and watch each player there. Ask yourself which players work the hardest. Observe how they practice and how they play in games. Do they push others to be better? Do they play with enthusiasm?

Out of all of the players you watch, choose only the ones that you think stand out as working harder than all the rest.

» How do the players you watched stand out? Why did you choose them?

» Would other players choose you as a hard worker? What would they say?

12

FREE YOUR MIND

Coaches and elite players often say that the game of basketball is just as much mental as it is physical. However, many players only practice the physical part of their game. They have not yet learned the importance of mental training.

Learn to increase your power of concentration by focusing your mind on a specific move. Your mind and body work together as one, so when you mentally think about a move that you want to make, your body will follow along.

Practice mental training by focusing on a single move. In your mind's eye, rehearse this move, over and over. See a perfect jump shot, one-on-one move, or game-winning free throw. The clearer the mental picture, the better your results will be.

I PICTURE A PERFECT
MOVE IN MY MIND.

PRACTICE THIS

This is an age-old exercise that quickly helps you to increase your ability to focus and concentrate. (For young players, make sure you have an adult's help.) Light a safe and secure candle with a flame that is easy to see. Place the candle on a table and sit in a chair next to it. Make sure you are at a safe distance. Next, look directly into the center of the flame. Do not strain your eyes; remember to blink! Concentrate on the flame for three minutes. Next, blow it out. Close your eyes and place the palms of your hands over your eyes. You will be able to see the flame inside the darkness of your closed eyes. Focus on the flame image until it fades into the darkness. Repeat once or twice a week until the image stays steady in the darkness without fading.

13

CONFIDENCE COMES FROM WITHIN

Sometimes you may feel that coaches are frustrated with you because you are not living up to their expectations. Or you may think that they are overlooking your talent and ability or not giving you enough support and encouragement. There may be times when you are just not getting along well with your teammates or family members.

There is no question that all players need coaches, parents, and teammates who have trust in them. That trust helps build confidence. However, when you are not getting a feeling of confidence from those around you, search for the kind that no one else can give you. Find the confidence that comes from within.

To have inner confidence, you must trust your skills, preparation, physical conditioning, and mental toughness. When you can honestly rely on these skills, you will feel extremely confident. It will show in the way you play because you know you have what it takes.

TRUSTING IN MY SKILLS
GIVES ME CONFIDENCE.

PRACTICE THIS

Write down every basketball skill that you possess, from the simplest to the most difficult. As you look at your list, put a plus (+) next to everything that you feel confident about. If you feel extremely confident, put a double-plus (++). Do not ask for anybody else's opinion; this has to come directly from you. If you are honest with yourself, all of those plusses will show just how confident you are about your game. When you find a skill or any other aspect that did not get a plus, do not lose heart. Instead, think of this as a challenge and an opportunity to improve and to eventually add more plusses to your list.

14

WELCOME PRESSURE

Coaches love players who thrive in pressure situations. Since playing under pressure is a big part of the game, coaches know that if their teams are going to have a chance, their players will have to channel the pressure they feel into poise and execution. However, the pressure of big games and competition in general can create intense anxiety because you may feel afraid that you won't get the job done. The expectations from your coaches, teammates, and sometimes even from parents and fans can get to you. All of the noise, excitement, and tension are a lot for anybody to deal with.

The fact is, you have made the choice and commitment to be a competitive athlete and will be playing regularly under this kind of pressure. You will be under the critical eyes of coaches, teammates, parents, and fans. Since pressure in basketball is unavoidable, why not accept it and let it help you play even better? Use the energy to bring out your competitive spirit. Say to yourself, "I *love* the pressure. Bring it on!"

I LOVE THE PRESSURE.
BRING IT ON!

CHRIS MULLIN AND TOM MITCHELL

PRACTICE THIS

The night before your next game, go into a room where you can be alone. Get into a comfortable position and relax. Then, imagine yourself in the gym where you will be playing. As you think about your upcoming game, you may feel some anxiety in your gut. That's okay! As the intensity within you begins to build, breathe into it. Continue to let the pressure grow. Excited and full of energy, see yourself playing exactly the way you want. Create a mental picture of success. As you keep breathing deeply, welcome that intensity, knowing that it will help make you a better player.

» What thoughts go through your mind when you are in intense pressure situations?

15

Beginner's Mind

When you first started playing basketball, you were eager to learn as much as you could. Your mind was open and your enthusiasm was at an all-time high. Being new to the sport, you wanted to improve every day. You looked forward to practice and games with excitement. You had the mind of a beginner.

Over time, things always change. You may put in many years of hard work and practice and have many different coaches. You will experience the highs and lows of winning and losing. You may even become a great player.

Have you ever noticed that some players have lost their kid-like enthusiasm? They forget how excited they once felt and why they loved playing basketball. Possibly, they become so good that they take their natural athletic abilities and their hard-earned skills for granted—and the passion starts to fade.

If you ever find this happening to you, remember why you fell in love with the game. Recall the enthusiasm and excitement you once felt on the court. Reawaken your innocence and think like a beginner again.

MY MIND IS OPEN. I LOVE
LEARNING NEW THINGS.

PRACTICE THIS

This is a good exercise if you have been playing basketball for some time. Whenever you feel overwhelmed with the pressure of competition or are just taking it all too seriously, find photos of yourself when you first started to play. Maybe you or others have kept a scrapbook of your various teams. Look at the first trophies, honors, or awards that you won. Possibly, you have video of your earliest games. Your earliest memories of basketball are important. Try to remember the excitement you had as a child. Recall how much fun you had and the good feelings that flooded you. Remember what it was like to be a beginner. Reawaken your joy for the game!

16

POSITIVE WORDS

Saying positive and encouraging words can help turn your dream into a reality. These are called *affirmations*: inspirational words or phrases that you say to yourself to help you remember your goal and train your mind to focus on what you want. When you use an affirmation, remember to keep it simple and speak to yourself in a natural way, as if you have already reached your goal.

Set goals that you feel are possible to reach, but don't limit yourself. It's good to set high standards and expect greatness. Think big! Say your words with feeling, meaning, and conviction.

Think of these words as if they were seeds being planted in your mind. With repetition and practice, these words will firmly take root and over time you will feel more positive and confident about reaching your goal.

I PUT POSITIVE WORDS AND
THOUGHTS IN MY MIND.

CHRIS MULLIN AND TOM MITCHELL

PRACTICE THIS

Imagine that a coach or another player you really respect comes up to you and tells you something very positive about yourself. Their compliments and encouraging words fill you with confidence. What did that person say? What qualities and skills impressed them so much?

» What are the most powerful words that you can say to yourself?

» What thoughts do you want to eliminate about yourself as a basketball player?

#3 | where to hit lay-ups |

#4 Defensive stance

(switch on screens)

[handwritten notes at top: "What do I need to / have I communicated? / #1 worl hard, do assignments / be in / #2 shape"]

17
TALK WITH YOUR COACH

Successful coaches have good communication skills. They impart their knowledge by using simple and direct words. When they explain things, you easily understand them. Their instructions are clear and you are able to apply them on the court. There is no confusion about what they expect from you.

Often, your coaches will communicate through body language or facial expressions. Sometimes, they give you a glance of confidence, a pat on the back, or a nod of approval.

You should learn to connect with your coach as well. At the right time, express your thoughts and let your coach or others know what is going on. Don't assume that they know what you are thinking or feeling or understand what you are going through.

Sometimes, it takes courage to speak directly to your coach because you may think that what you have to say will be rejected. But eventually in life, you will need to speak up for yourself. Why not start now? Practice communicating clearly about what you think and feel is important.

The one reason I'M such a successful coach is I ~~have~~ have 1 way to do everything!

I LET MY COACH KNOW WHAT IS GOING ON IN MY LIFE.

The reason I'M failing in other areas of life is that Ambiguity isn't level of mere!

PRACTICE THIS

The next time you feel concerned or confused about something that involves your coach (or anyone else, for that matter), ask for some time when you can sit down and talk about what is on your mind. You may want to write down your thoughts before the meeting so that you will remember everything you want to say. Be truthful and honest when you talk, but also be respectful. If you do this whenever it is needed, your relationship will grow and you will find it easier to communicate in the future.

» What would you like to talk about with your coach?

» Is there anybody else you need to talk with? What do you want to say?

18

Your Inner Circle

As a basketball player, you are involved in a very competitive sport. You will face tough opponents. You will be evaluated at each level. Other coaches will form opinions about you and comment on your talent, athletic ability, and skill to perform under pressure situations. Fans and others may talk about you; sometimes they'll say good things, sometimes bad.

It is natural for you to care about what others think. But the only opinions that *really* matter are those from people who have your best interest at heart—your inner circle: coaches, teammates, family members, and true friends.

However, people who hardly know you will make comments about you. If they are negative criticisms, it can be very tough to let these opinions roll off your back. Nevertheless, try not to put value in the opinions of people who don't even know you. This will make a big difference in how you play and feel about yourself.

THE PEOPLE IN MY INNER CIRCLE HAVE MY BACK.

PRACTICE THIS

On a sheet of paper, draw a large circle. Then write the names of the people who really care about you. Put them at different locations within the circle.

Whenever you hear negative comments, decide if those critics are members of this inner circle. If those comments *do* come from your inner circle, listen carefully to them because you can trust where they are coming from. There may be something said that you need to hear.

If they do not come from members of your inner circle, ask yourself, "Do these people *really* want me to succeed? Do they *really* have my back?" If not, turn your attention away from their comments and free yourself from their critical and potentially harmful words.

19

EMOTIONS ARE REAL

After preparing for a big game, your expectations are high and you want to play your best. You know that your team can win. And when you *do* play well and win, you feel excited and happy.

But what happens when you don't play as well as expected or you lose? Maybe your team is out of sync. Maybe you make some mental errors or just can't buy a basket. Maybe another player dominates you. Whatever happens, you walk off of the court feeling the loss and no words of encouragement can comfort you.

Yes, many times things won't go your way and you must learn to walk away with your chin up. But at the right time and place it's okay to show your feelings and let your emotions out. Your emotions are real. You hurt because you care. Sometimes, you need to tell somebody how you feel. Once in a while, shedding a tear may be the healthiest thing that you can do because it helps to wash away your pain. Emotions are part of the game. Letting your feelings out allows you to move on.

EMOTIONS ARE REAL AND PART OF BEING AN ATHLETE.

PRACTICE THIS

"Mad, Sad, and Glad" is a powerful exercise in which you get to express a wide range of emotions.

Write down things involving basketball that have made you really *mad*. Next, write something that has made you feel *sad*. Finally, write something that makes you really *glad*.

> » How does competing with some emotion help you play better?

20

Right Here, Right Now

Sometimes you will hear players talking about their future. They seem to think that the next level is where the "big time" is. Don't be fooled. Never let your search for the gold in the future blind you to the treasures in the present. Right here is the best place for you and right now is the best time.

It also seems strange when you hear a player talking about his past with a sense of longing to somehow get it back. It seems that a part of him yearns for the time when he was playing for the love of it and when basketball was more meaningful.

Although it is good to have goals and aspire to higher levels in the game, remember that the best place and time for you is in the present moment. Take a look around and see all that you have. Appreciate your present level of play. Your upcoming game is just as important as anybody else's. Your practice today is just as important as that of the best players in the world. Enjoy yourself and be glad to be where you are.

THE BEST PLACE IS
RIGHT WHERE I AM.

PRACTICE THIS

Each time you find yourself worrying about your future, wasting unnecessary energy by wondering what's going to happen, say to yourself, "Right here, right now."

Likewise, if you find yourself thinking about past mistakes and wishing that you could do it all over again, say to yourself, "Right here, right now."

This simple yet powerful exercise, if practiced over and over, trains your mind to think in the present moment. Your attention focuses in the "here and now" and you get rid of useless thoughts about things that you can't control.

> » How do you feel when you're completely
>   absorbed in the moment?

My love for the game of basketball created a powerful drive within me; playing with my brothers for hours on end, sneaking into the gym at midnight to practice my shooting, and keeping my body in shape was just what I did and who I was. And although I am proud of my accomplishments, I am even more grateful for the people I have met, the friends I have made, and the lessons I have learned along the way.

CHRIS MULLIN AND TOM MITCHELL

Although I have had my share of achievements, my life has not been without some very difficult struggles and tough challenges. I've had to deal with both personal and professional setbacks.

Basketball and life in general hasn't always been easy. I've had to work extra hard to make up for my limitations both on and off the court. I've had to take a hard look at myself, and become clear about what I believe in and the things I stand for.

I like to think back to some of the early basketball life lessons I was taught. I learned that there was a right and wrong way to do things on the court. I learned that my attitude was a choice. It was within my control to work hard. I wanted to exceed my own expectations and hold myself to a higher standard.

I feel very fortunate to have played with some of the greatest basketball players of all time. Being selected as a member of the 1992 USA Olympic Team (the original Dream Team) with teammates such as Magic Johnson, Larry Bird, and Michael Jordan was one of the highlights of my career. Sometimes I would ask myself, "How was it that I was able to earn a spot on the best basketball team ever assembled?"

My first thoughts always go to the people in my life who were at the core of my success: my mother and father, brothers, sister, coaches, and certain teammates. These were the people who always had my best interest at heart, no matter what.

Tom and I first started talking about the topics in our book while shooting around in his backyard in the mid-90s.

21

Have Courage

There may be situations that arise on or off the court that are difficult to deal with. Often, the difficulty comes from a lack of communication or a misunderstanding between you and someone else.

If the problem is with a coach, teammate, friend, or a member of your family, remember that these are the people you need to have healthy relationships with. Work through the conflict and create a positive feeling between you and the other person. Confront these tough situations so everyone can clear the air and you can focus on basketball as well as all the other important aspects of your life.

Sometimes it is difficult to bring up sensitive issues. But if you want to have a solid relationship, you must be willing to talk. Have courage and take time to work things out. Find a place where you can be alone and can talk face to face. Get your feelings off your chest. Be as direct and honest as possible. Listen well and be ready to hear what the other person has to say.

I HAVE THE COURAGE TO DEAL
WITH TOUGH SITUATIONS.

CHRIS MULLIN AND TOM MITCHELL

PRACTICE THIS

Observe how people you know deal with difficult situations. You may find that many people say they are going to clear the air with someone, but when it comes down to it, they can't find the courage to discuss their disagreements, frustrations, or challenges.

When you find people who are brave enough to confront tough situations head-on, ask them how they do it. Ask them how they find the courage to not back down and have the strength to work things out.

» What situation or person in your life is difficult to deal with? How are you dealing with it?
» What is the toughest situation you ever had to deal with?

22

Express Yourself

Although nobody likes to hear players bragging about their accomplishments, if you are a good player, there is nothing wrong with knowing it. If you are a good player, it means you have put a lot of time and dedication into basketball and have confidence in your game. You know that you are tough in pressure situations and have proven your ability to lead your team.

When you are feeling good about your game, and you can play at a high level, there is no need to hide it. When you walk into any gym, knowing that you belong there, a quiet confidence flows from you. When you know you are a talented player and can prove it, others can sense your competitive fire. In times like these, it's natural to be proud of yourself. It's good to feel like a champ. You've earned it!

I AM PROUD OF WHO I AM
AND WHAT I HAVE EARNED.

PRACTICE THIS

Put on your favorite music and sit down with a piece of paper. Make a list of everything that you like about yourself. Really get into it. Don't be shy. After all, it's *your life!* Anything and everything that you like and appreciate about yourself should be included.

» How can you be proud of yourself, yet not let it go to your head?

» What do you think "quiet confidence" means?

23

HAVE FUN

It has been said that there is no substitute for hard work, and this is very true. Yet it is also true that playing basketball should be fun. Sure, it is important to develop good work habits and concentrate on improving skills. But remember, you first fell in love with the game because of how fun it was.

As you become a more committed player, the pressures in a season can squeeze the fun out of the game. Sometimes, you may even get tired of practice. Basketball becomes more of a job than a joy; it feels more like work than play.

If you ever feel this way, remember the kid in you who was once so excited about playing. Even if you are a very successful player, don't forget that basketball is a game and play for the fun of it. When you run, shoot, dribble, pass, jump, slide, and defend, do so with an enthusiastic spirit. Enjoy feeling healthy, strong, and young. Feel the kid within you. Let go of all your cares and play the game.

PLAYING BASKETBALL IS ONE OF
THE BEST FEELINGS IN THE WORLD!

PRACTICE THIS

Take a moment to remember some of the favorite basketball games you used to play. They could be the games that you learned in your backyard, or at the park, or at summer camp.

For example, can you remember having fun playing one-on-one with a friend? How about knock out, dribble tag, horse, or around the world? Possibly, you played with your opposite hand or made up some of your own games.

Find some friends or teammates and just play for the fun of it. The games that can still bring out the kid in you and put a smile on your face should become part of your weekly routine. They will loosen you up, release some pressure, and reawaken your enthusiasm for basketball.

24

THE INNER COACH

As a basketball player, you are constantly getting information from outside sources. For example, you are constantly receiving instruction and information from coaches. Or you may get advice from older players. Sometimes, you will pick up information while watching basketball on TV, or from reading basketball books and magazines.

Probably the most important source of basketball information and inspiration is from your coaches. Their jobs are to help you develop your skill, conditioning, and competitive spirit. Listen carefully to them.

However, it is also important to know the coach within yourself. All of us have a presence inside us that can give us direction and guidance when it's needed. This is sometimes called the voice of the inner coach.

Become close to your inner coach. Listen to its message as it supports and encourages you. In your own private way, become aware of this mighty force within you.

I LISTEN TO THE
COACH WITHIN ME.

PRACTICE THIS

The next time you find yourself lacking confidence, feeling confused, or needing a solution to a problem, go to a favorite place where you can be alone and you can have a conversation with yourself as if you were talking with your best friend. Tell yourself what is going on and what you are feeling. Don't hold anything back.

Ask yourself for direction so that you can clearly see what steps you need to take. Allow a few minutes of silence to pass as you listen for a message or an answer from within.

» What would be the most important thing your inner coach would want you to know?

25

Beyond the Score

As a competitive player, you know that your team will either win or lose the game. The score and standings will be kept. Naturally, you want to win. The desire to win shows that you have a strong competitive drive and you take pride in your game. But there are no guarantees of winning the game. Who knows? You may face a better team with better players. Possibly, you will play the best game of your life and still not win.

However, giving it everything you've got is a form of success, too. When you and your teammates play with heart and give great effort, you can walk away with your head up, no matter what the final score is.

If having more points than the other team is the only important thing to you, you set yourself up for disappointment every time you step on the court. If the final score is the only thing that matters, feeling good about yourself and the team depends on the final result rather than your effort.

Instead of worrying so much about the score, why not focus on what *is* under your control? Concentrate on making others around you better and doing all the things you worked on in practice.

I GIVE IT MY ALL, MENTALLY
AND PHYSICALLY.

PRACTICE THIS

Before your next game, take some time to be alone. For a few minutes, don't even care if you win or lose. Instead, think, "In today's game, I will give my best effort. I will give everything I have, mentally and physically. I will help make my teammates better."

When the game is over, see if you feel satisfied with your effort. If the answer is yes, and you really mean it, be proud of yourself regardless of the final score. Feel good that you stayed focused and played the right way.

» Did you ever play really well but not win the game? How did you feel?
» Can you focus on playing and not worry so much about the final score?

26

FEAR AS AN ADVANTAGE

Understanding your fear can be a huge advantage. Every competitive basketball player deals with fear. This is not to suggest that living in a constant state of fear is healthy. Too much fear will rob you of your confidence, causing you to over-think and tighten up. However, having some fear in the competitive arena can be good.

In basketball, there are plenty of things to fear. There is always the possibility of hurting your body. Also, when you play in front of a crowd, you run the risk of publicly making mistakes, losing, or being criticized.

Learn to use fear to your advantage. Pay attention to the situation you are afraid of and ask yourself, "Why am I afraid?" If you are afraid of getting injured, accept that possibility and become more alert and aware of your surroundings. If you are afraid of losing, know that this will happen sometimes. When it does, learn and move on, looking forward to your next game. If you are afraid of criticism, get ready to hear it and use it for inspiration to get better.

I AM LEARNING TO FACE FEARS HEAD-ON AND USE THEM TO MY ADVANTAGE.

PRACTICE THIS

If you ever find yourself having a bad case of pre-game jitters, find a place where you can be alone for 5 to 10 minutes. Then, imagine that the very thing that you fear *does* happen. Picture losing the game or choking on the free throw line! Bring what you fear most out in the open. When you do so, *you* gain power over it. No matter what happens, you will still have yourself, your confidence, and your love for the game—the things that can't be taken from you. Now imagine playing in the game again. This time, see everything happening just the way you want. Visualize the outcome you desire.

- » What is the advantage of facing your fear?
- » After facing your fear, why is it important to go back and visualize a positive outcome?

27

LEARN FROM LOSS

Playing basketball has its risks. When you play, you run the risk of getting hurt. Basketball is a physically demanding game. To excel, you need to be tough.

Also, you run the risk of being embarrassed by making mistakes in front of other players and spectators. If you play long enough, you will not escape being humbled. Although you may want to play your best all the time, you could temporarily lose your courage to perform in the clutch. You could be the player who turns the ball over in crunch time or misses a free throw that would have won the game. You may feel like you have let your coach and team down.

When you have a bad game, let your disappointment be the fuel that gives you even more motivation to improve. Think about the things you want to work on in practice and the lessons you have learned from your loss.

It is okay to feel the pain of losing or frustration of failing, but don't dwell on it too long. When you lose a game or make a critical mistake, take the time to learn from it and then move on.

I LEARN FROM MY LOSS
AND MOVE ON.

PRACTICE THIS

Think about the biggest mistake or disappointment you have experienced in basketball. It could have to do with losing a big game, choking under pressure, messing up an assignment, or even sitting on the bench and not getting into a game.

» With each heart-breaking loss, one learns a lesson. What lesson did you learn?
» How does losing or failing give you greater determination?

28

PROTECT YOURSELF

In the world of basketball, there are going to be times when you need to protect yourself. People will attack your confidence from time to time. For example, someone may be jealous of your success and may attempt to rob you of your enthusiasm and confidence. His or her criticism may cause you to seriously doubt your abilities.

If this happens to you, stand firm and protect yourself. Although your feelings may be shaken, nobody can rob you of your confidence; *it is based on you trusting your proven skill and talent.* And, unless you allow it, nobody can rob you of your enthusiasm.

There is greatness within you. Self-worth does not depend on what others say or think. Build a protective shield around yourself with positive and encouraging words. Using your imagination, surround your body with courage as if it was a cloak. Remind yourself that there is a champion within you.

I PROTECT MYSELF.
NOBODY CAN STEAL
MY CONFIDENCE.

PRACTICE THIS

Using the power of your mind, imagine a protective force field surrounding your body. Give it a color, a size, and a shape. Visualize it encircling and protecting you.

The next time you are in a situation when something has a negative influence on you, use this technique to protect yourself. Imagine that your protective force field is blocking out everything that is not helpful so that you can remain positive and confident.

» How does it feel to be surrounded by an imaginary protective force field?
» What does it look like?

29

WALK IN THEIR SHOES

In basketball, compassion and humility are not often talked about. After all, you compete against other players and everyone wants to win. You are *not* usually taught to put yourself in someone else's shoes. You are trained to think mainly about your own team and personal success.

However, you can be a fierce, competitive basketball player and still be a compassionate person. You can treat other players and other people the same way you would like to be treated. You can be gracious when you win by understanding what the losing team is going through.

When you have humility, you care about more than just your own success. Although you may be a superior player, you don't think of yourself as being more important than anyone else. You look for the good in everyone. You radiate kindness and respectfulness: qualities that are at the heart of true champions.

I TREAT OTHER PLAYERS THE WAY I WANT TO BE TREATED.

PRACTICE THIS

When you see other players having a tough time, this is an opportunity for you to practice a little compassion. From your own experience, you know that there are many things that can cause players to feel down—a tough loss, a bad game, not playing, getting in trouble with a coach, or any number of personal problems.

The best thing you can do is to simply ask if they are okay and if there is anything you can do to help. Be a superior listener. You don't have to give advice or offer solutions. Just let them tell you what they are thinking and feeling. Show that you care; sometimes, that's all it takes.

> » Who was there for you during your toughest times?

30

EVALUATE YOURSELF

It's an important step in your development as a basketball player to evaluate yourself. Asking yourself honest questions about your physical and mental skills will help clarify where you stand. You will discover your strengths and weaknesses and have a better understanding of who you really are as an athlete.

Identifying your strengths will build your confidence and self-esteem. When you know the things you do well, it helps you become a better player. It gives you greater trust in your ability.

Identifying your weaknesses also helps you improve your game. Knowing your limitations will make you more determined and committed to work even harder.

When you evaluate yourself, be completely honest. Self-critique is essential to self-improvement.

KNOWING BOTH MY STRENGTHS
AND WEAKNESSES MAKES
ME A BETTER PLAYER.

PRACTICE THIS

With complete honesty, ask the following questions about yourself as a basketball player:

» What are my strengths?
» Where do I need to improve?
» Am I a coach's dream?
» Do I practice with intensity?
» What kind of shape am I in?
» Do I love playing under pressure?

Do this exercise regularly. Record your answers in a journal. It will be interesting for you to see how your answers change in the weeks, months, and years to come.

31

PLAYING IN THE MOMENT

Basketball provides you the opportunity to play fully in the present moment. If you recall when you first started playing, you put all of your concentration into what you were doing. You were not worried about the past or the future. You just wanted to be on the court. You were playing "in the moment."

Past accomplishments are as important as future goals. They both serve a purpose. However, try not to dwell too much on your past success or mistakes; they're behind you. And try not to worry too much about the future; it's not here yet!

When you are playing basketball and bring your full attention into the present moment, you are aware of what is happening on the court *right now*—and what you need to do. When you learn to bring your mind fully into the now, you feel under control. You play the game with poise and confidence.

I AM FOCUSED AND AWARE OF
WHAT IS HAPPENING
ON THE COURT.

CHRIS MULLIN AND TOM MITCHELL

PRACTICE THIS

When you are practicing alone, pretend that the clock is running down and you only have a few seconds to make your move and score. Create the feeling of game pressure. Practice making the game-winning shot over and over, each time feeling the pressure like you were in a real game.

Try this with different offensive moves. Each time create the feeling of pressure and then take and make a big shot.

» What does it feel like when you take and make the game-winning shot?

32

A Powerful Imagination

When you use your imagination, you can see things in your mind's eye before they actually happen. You can see yourself hitting a big shot, making a pass, breaking a press, or shutting down a player on defense.

Learn to use your imagination and let it help you with your game. Think about something you want to accomplish on the court and then see yourself doing it. Daydream as long as you want about every aspect of basketball. When you see yourself playing well in your mind, that image will build confidence when you to go for it on the court.

Before each game, pretend that you are on the court, playing the way you want. See yourself running, shooting, jumping, passing, and defending with confidence and control. With your vivid imagination visualize your game, both offensively and defensively. When you see it, you will believe it and then can achieve it.

I CAN SEE IT IN MY MIND AND
ACHIEVE IT ON THE COURT.

PRACTICE THIS

First, write down something that you *really* want to achieve . . . a goal or dream that you really want to come true.

Next, draw a picture of your goal. Draw as much detail into this picture as possible. Imagine the colors, the sounds, the entire environment.

Finally, close your eyes and pretend that this very goal does come true. Let your imagination run wild and experience your future goal happening in the present moment.

» Can you imagine what you really want to achieve on the court?
» How does using your imagination help you to play better?

33

RELAX . . .

Many of us live fast-paced lives, racing from activity to activity. We want to do well on the court and still have time for other interests. All too often, we feel the anxiety of falling behind. Even though finding time to recharge may not seem to fit into your busy schedule, relaxing is important.

Some competitive tension is good and can help you play with more focus, but too much can cause you to tighten up and lose your rhythm and flow. Relaxation calms you down.

Relaxation is healthy for your mind and body. When you enter into a state of relaxation, your muscles loosen and revitalizing energy flows through you. You feel refreshed. Stress fades and your mind becomes quiet.

There are many ways to relax. You can listen to music, soak in hot water, or just sit quietly. Both stretching and deep breathing will help you become really calm. The important thing is that you find a method that works and make time to recharge.

WHEN I RELAX, MY BODY
AND MIND RECHARGE.

PRACTICE THIS

Find a place where you can be undisturbed. Get into a comfortable position, sitting in a chair with your hands on your knees or folded in your lap. Keeping your back straight and your feet firmly on the floor, relax your shoulders and close your eyes. As you settle in, watch your breathing. Allow your breaths to become full and deep and notice the air moving in and out. When thoughts pop into your head, guide your attention back to your breathing. Slow, deep breathing will help you relax.

Continue taking slow, deep breaths for several minutes until you sink into a feeling of calmness.

34

NEVER GIVE UP

When you talk to elite players about what has made them so successful, they will often talk about their determination. They understand the importance of having an iron will. They know that committed players rise to the top.

When you are a determined basketball player, your desire does not lessen in time; it burns steadily, day in and day out. You have a strong will and unwavering conviction. When things get tough, as they sometimes do, having a determined spirit will help you through the difficulty. If you experience a setback in your game or have a physical injury, being determined will help you overcome it.

Be consistent and steadfast in your desire to achieve, no matter how difficult the challenge. Fight for your dream. Never give up!

I FIGHT FOR MY DREAM
AND NEVER GIVE UP.

PRACTICE THIS

Recall a time in your life when you had a big challenge ahead. Possibly there was something getting in your way and the odds of success seemed to be against you. Maybe others around you didn't believe you could succeed, but within you was a fierce power of determination. You knew that you could do it—and you did! Remember how you tapped into that power and how it drove you to succeed?

» How did you tap into your spirit of determination?
» What big challenge are you currently facing?

35

APPRECIATE IT ALL

Serious and dedicated basketball players set high standards for themselves. Once players reach a certain level, they usually want to move on to an even higher one. It is extremely rewarding for committed players to see how far they can take their game.

However, every now and then, it's not a bad idea to just appreciate what you have and how much you have already accomplished. Appreciate what good shape you are in and the skills you have developed. Be grateful that you are part of such a tremendous sport and the thrill and intensity of competition it offers. Be thankful for your coaches, family, teammates, and friends that you have made. Especially appreciate the free time you have to practice and play. Look around and you'll be amazed at how much you have going for you right now!

It is good to want more. Just make sure to take some time to appreciate what you already have.

I FEEL FORTUNATE TO HAVE
BASKETBALL IN MY LIFE.

CHRIS MULLIN AND TOM MITCHELL

PRACTICE THIS

Before falling asleep, lie down and think about all of the good things that have come your way because of basketball. Before you drift off, feel how incredibly fortunate you are to have basketball in your life.

Appreciate all that you have right now—all of your skills and knowledge about the game; all of your accomplishments, both big and small; your teammates and coaches; the hours you have spent practicing; and the joy that you have felt while playing.

» It's fun to create a collage of some of your favorite basketball pictures of the past. You can paste photos of your home court, teammates, coaches, family members, and important others.

36

Ask for Help

As you strive to improve your game, you will need lots of help along the way. Hopefully, you will have a supportive family and good communication with your coach. However, coaches can be busy helping their other players. Your parents have jobs and many responsibilities to think about. Sometimes, those people closest to you may be unaware of something that is bothering you.

Don't expect the people closest to you to be able to read your mind. Whenever you feel troubled or confused about something, ask for help. There is no sense in ignoring what you are going through or thinking that a problem will just go away. Sometimes, another point of view from someone you trust and respect is exactly what's needed. Asking for help is a big step in your personal growth.

If you need extra help on the court, make sure that your coaches know about it. They may think that everything is just fine, but really you may be frustrated or seriously questioning yourself. Don't be afraid to share your struggles.

I ASK FOR HELP FROM PEOPLE
I TRUST AND RESPECT.

PRACTICE THIS

Ask yourself if there is anything going on that you could use some extra help with. Are you struggling with an aspect of your game? Are you feeling frustrated or lacking some confidence? Is anything else going on in your life that is causing you to lose some of your direction and motivation? Do you need some help?

If so, identify people who can help. Have the courage to ask for advice. When you do get sound advice, make sure that you really understand it. Then, put this knowledge and advice into practice and see what happens.

> » Who has really helped you when you needed it?
> » Is it easy for you to ask for help?

37

GO BEYOND YOUR COMFORT ZONE

There are some days when playing comes easily. You feel quick and have good reactions. You play with intensity. You have focus and energy, making strong moves to the basket. Your shot feels great. You make good decisions and the game just seems to come to you. This is known as "the zone."

Playing in the zone happens when your game comes together into a flow. It feels like you will never get tired. Sometimes your body feels light and the game seems to move slower than usual. You play with both creativity and control.

However, no one consistently plays in the zone. There will be days when it is difficult to find enough energy to go to practice. You may be tired, distracted, or unprepared.

This is when you need to apply extra effort. With concentration, discipline, and will power, you must find a way to give it everything you have and challenge yourself to push beyond your comfort zone. When you train yourself to give this kind of effort, there is no telling what you can achieve.

I DIG IN AND PUSH BEYOND
MY COMFORT ZONE.

PRACTICE THIS

Pick a practice day when you find it hard to concentrate and be full of energy—a day when you really don't even want to go to practice.

Make a commitment to yourself that on that day you will take your practice to another level. No matter how you feel or what is going on around you, challenge yourself to practice with greater concentration and intensity and push beyond your comfort zone.

»   How does it feel to really "dig in" and push yourself when you are not feeling your best?

38

CELEBRATE SUCCESS

It feels good when you play well and your team wins. It feels even better when you reach a goal that you have been striving towards all season long. When you stop and think about the time, effort, and dedication that you have put into basketball, it's impressive!

Your good fortune has not come easily. The team and personal success you experience is a statement about you, about the commitment you made and what you have given up for basketball. Your victories did not happen overnight, but rather after weeks and months of hard work.

Take time to enjoy your team accomplishments and celebrate your success. Be proud of what you have earned and enjoy it for a while before moving on to your next challenge. Give your teammates and yourself a pat on the back. You all deserve it!

I LOVE CELEBRATING
WITH MY TEAMMATES!

PRACTICE THIS

The next time your team plays well and wins, go out of your way to enjoy it even more than usual. For example, you can take a moment with your coaches and thank them for the job they did (this may surprise them, but even coaches need praise from time to time). Or make the time to tell your teammates what an awesome job they have done.

» What are some favorite ways you celebrate? Where do you go? What do you do?

39

GIVING BACK

No matter what your age, if you have been a serious basketball player for a while, you have most likely gained valuable knowledge about your sport. You have learned how to practice and prepare for games. You understand the meaning of desire and dedication. You have developed sound skills, strong work habits, and the ability to focus.

To continue growing as a person as well as an athlete, it is important that you give back what you know to others. There will always be beginning players who want to be able to do what you do on the court. They may end up loving basketball just like you.

You don't need to be a coach to share what you know with others. Nor do you need to be an expert. At the right time and place and in a friendly and caring way, give back some of the same positive energy, knowledge, and enthusiasm that was given to you. It is often said that the best way to master something is to teach it to others. When you do this, you are completing a cycle of giving and receiving.

I ENJOY GIVING BACK
WHAT I HAVE LEARNED.

PRACTICE THIS

Find a younger or less skilled basketball player who really wants to learn about the game. It could even be with a complete beginner. Once you are on the court together and you can see their level of play, show them a basic skill or game you know.

For example, you could demonstrate layups, ball handling, passing, or shooting. Depending on their skill level, you could teach more advanced things. Make it fun and positive, with lots of encouragement. Keep in mind that it's about them and not you. By taking time to share your basketball knowledge with someone else, you'll feel really good about yourself. Who knows, you may become a coach someday.

> » Who are the best coaches you've ever had? What made them so good?

40

HONOR THE GAME

There are so many great things about basketball. Playing it teaches important lessons and provides you with memories that will last a lifetime. For example:

» You develop confidence and self-discipline.
» You become strong and physically fit.
» You get to play in front of a crowd.
» You do something that is really fun.
» You learn how to deeply concentrate and focus.
» You learn to develop courage under pressure.
» You make friends with other players.
» You share in the great spirit of competition.

What else gives you all of this? Isn't basketball great?

BASKETBALL IS THE BEST!

CHRIS MULLIN AND TOM MITCHELL

PRACTICE THIS

The next time that you have a paper to write or a speech to give, do it about basketball. This will be an easy assignment because there is so much to write or talk about.

Hearing your basketball stories will interest your audience. They will be able to feel your enthusiasm and passion for the game. When you talk about your experiences and lessons, whoever is listening or reading your words will feel your love for the game.

» How has reading this book helped your game?
» What have you learned about yourself as a person?

Acknowledgements

The authors would like to extend their thanks to the members of our production team:

Charles L. Darr
Editorial Consultant

Charles has spent his professional career teaching writing, literature, and humanities at the university level. He is Professor Emeritus at The University of Pittsburgh at Johnstown, Pennsylvania.

Sam Forencich
Photographer

Sam—a commercial freelance photographer specializing in NBA images from the San Francisco Bay Area and, of late, Portland, Oregan—may be contacted by e-mail at sam@samforencich.com.